Things You Should NEVER Do

Ed Morrow

CONTEMPORARY
BOOKS
A TRIBUNE NEW MEDIA COMPANY

Library of Congress Cataloging-in-Publication Data

Morrow, Ed.
    599 things you should never do / Ed Morrow.
        p.   cm.
    ISBN 0-8092-3368-1
    1. Quotations.   2. Quotations, English.
I. Title
PN6081.M575   1995
082—dc20   95-32604
                                              CIP

Illustrations by Ed Morrow

Published by Contemporary Books, Inc.
Two Prudential Plaza, Chicago, Illinois 60601-6790
Manufactured in the United States of America
International Standard Book Number: 0-8092-3368-1
10   9   8   7   6   5   4   3   2   1

CONTENTS

ACKNOWLEDGMENTS

Once again, I must thank my wife, Laurie. She never failed to offer me the support and help without which this book would never have been completed. I can never thank her enough.

I also must thank Sheree Bykofsky, who never ceases to give me the professional advice and aid that makes her the best literary agent a writer could hope for.

I would also like to thank Linda Gray and Gerilee Hundt at Contemporary Books for their hard work and encouragement.

INTRODUCTION

Wouldn't it be nice if there were a few absolute rules that could be used to navigate life's harrowing shoals? Wouldn't Tom Arnold feel better if he had embraced P. G. Wodehouse's advice "Never have yourself tattooed with any woman's name, not even her initials"? Now, with this handy compendium of wise and witty admonitions, never again will the hapless be without guidance.

Have you spotted the girl of your dreams at the end of the bar? Here's a thought: "Never try to pick up a woman who is wearing a Super Bowl ring" (Garry Shandling). Planning to take a pleasure trip? "Never say

'Hi Jack' in an airport" (Terry Denton). Perhaps you're contemplating a life of crime. With this book, you'll know how to avoid an all-too-common mistake. "Never steal anything so small that you'll have to go to an unpleasant city jail for it instead of a minimum-security federal tennis prison" (P. J. O'Rourke).

Whether you're looking for etiquette tips ("Never hit a man with glasses. Hit him with something bigger and heavier"), a new diet plan ("Never eat more than you can lift"), or a reassuring affirmation of life's great possibilities ("Never believe that things can't get worse"), *599 Things You Should Never Do* is your guide to all the no-nos, big and small, that should never be ignored.

ACADEMIA

"Never consult the economics department.
. . . never consult the business school."

> *Paul A. Samuelson, Nobel Prize–
> winning economist, quoting a former
> Harvard treasurer*

ACHIEVEMENT

"Never rode; never fell."

> *Old English adage, traced to 1537*

"Never forget. . . . the best way to keep people away from you is not to be good at anything. There's so many people who could be good, could be great, if they tried. . . . Some people are scared to risk it, though. Me, I say, 'If you're scared, buy a dog.' "

> *Charles Barkley (1963–),*
> *basketball star,* Vanity Fair,
> *February 1995*

"Never measure the height of a mountain until you have reached the top. Then you will see how low it was."

> *Dag Hammarskjöld (1905–1960), U.N.*
> *Secretary General and recreational*
> *mountaineer,* Markings, *1964*

"Never consent to creep when one feels an impulse to soar."

> *Helen Keller (1880–1968)*

"Never try and you'll never know."

Emma Morrow (1917–1979)

"Never face facts; if you do you'll never get up in the morning."

Marlo Thomas (1943–   ), actress, as quoted by Merrit Malloy and Shauna Sorensen in The Quotable Quote Book, *1990*

"Never assume you'll be turned down."

Joan Rivers (1937–   ), on auditioning

"Never let that bastard back in here— unless we need him."

Adolph Zukor, filmmaker, attributed (also attributed to Samuel Goldwyn, Harry M. Warner, and other moviemakers)

ACTING AND SHOW BUSINESS

"Never work with animals or kids."

> *W. C. Fields (1879–1946), attributed*

"Never cheat. . . . work your best and work your hardest and they'll respond to you."

> *Judy Garland (1922–1969)*

"Never trust anybody in show business."

> *Jonathan Harris, as Dr. Zachary Smith in "Lost in Space"*

ACTION

"Never worry about action, but only about inaction."

> *Winston Churchill (1874–1965)*

"Never take a course of action on the sole ground that reprehensible people are urging the opposite course."

D. Sutton, as quoted by John W. Gardner and Frencesca Gardner Reese in Know or Listen to Those Who Know, *1975*

ADULTERY

"Never tell. Not if you love your wife—in fact, if your old lady walks in on you, deny it. Yeah. Just flat out and she'll believe it. I'm tellin' ya."

Lenny Bruce (1926–1966), as quoted in The Essential Lenny Bruce, *edited by J. Cohen, 1967*

"Never approach a friend's girlfriend or wife with mischief as your goal. There are just too many women in the world to justify that sort of dishonorable behavior. Unless she's *really* attractive."

> *Bruce Jay Friedman (1930–),*
> *"Sex and the Lonely Guy,"* Esquire,
> *1977*

ADVICE

"Never say you don't know—nod wisely, leave calmly, then run like hell to find the nearest expert."

> *S. M. Oddo*

"Never whisper to the deaf or wink at the blind."

> *Slovenian adage*

"Never give advice in a crowd."

> *Arab adage*

AGE

"Never grow up completely, because that is when you start getting old."

> *Roger Clinton (1957–   )*

"Never tell your age."

> *A young mother to her baby girl in a Bac*Os television ad, 1994*

"Never trust anyone over thirty."

> *Jerry Rubin (1939–1994), quoting David Weinberger, in Growing (Up) at 37, 1976*

"Never tell the truth to an old woman. Especially when she asks for it."

Pharaoh's mother, The Egyptian (1954)

"Never ask old people how they are if you have anything else to do that day."

Joe Restivo, as quoted by Robert Byrne in The Fourth and by Far the Most Recent 637 Best Things Anybody Ever Said, *1990*

"Never trust a woman who tells her real age. If she tells that, she'll tell anything."

Oscar Wilde (1854–1900), A Woman of No Importance, *1893*

"Never lose sight of the fact that old age needs so little, but needs that little so much."

Margaret Willour

AIR TRAVEL

Never Say "Hi Jack" in an Airport

> *Title of a book on traveling by Terry Denton, 1993*

ALCOHOL

"Never drink anything stronger than you are."

> *Anonymous*

"Never trust a man who says he doesn't drink."

> *Anonymous drinker*

"Never be photographed holding a cocktail glass."

> *H. Jackson Brown, Jr.*

"Never drink when you are wretched without it. . . . drink when you would be happy without it."

> G. K. Chesterton (1874–1936)

"Never drink anything stronger than gin before breakfast."

> W. C. Fields (1879–1946)

"Never give black coffee to an intoxicated person. You may wind up with a wide-awake drunk on your hands."

> Ann Landers (1918–   ), in a
> preholiday advice column,
> December 3, 1993

"Never drink ardent spirit, even temporarily; for all drunkards were once temperate drinkers."

The Old Farmer's Almanac, 1834, as reprinted in The Best of The Old Farmer's Almanac, edited by Judson Hale. Hale noted that a few pages away from the page that carried this stern warning was a chart giving the distances from one "established tavern" to another all across New England.

"Never pour good liquor after bad."

Prohibition era adage

"Never have a small glass of port, my lad. It just goes wambling around looking for damage to do. Have a large glass. It settles down and does you good."

Lord Goddard, to a young member of his club, as quoted by Frank Pepper in The Wit and Wisdom of the 20th Century, 1987

"Never cry over spilt milk. It could've been whiskey."

> *James Garner (1928–   ) as Bret Maverick, quoting Pappy Maverick in "Maverick"*

"Never consume anything that's been aged in a radiator."

> *David Ogden Stiers, as Maj. Charles Emerson Winchester III, "M*A*S*H"*

"Never trust ale from a God-fearing people. . . ."

> *Quark, "Deep Space Nine"*

AMERICA

"Never sell America short."

> *Bumper sticker*

"Never lose faith in America. Its faults are yours to fix, not to curse."

Colin L. Powell (1937–   )

ANGER

"Never act when you're angry."

Fortune cookie

"Never forget what a man says to you when he is angry."

Henry Ward Beecher (1813–1887)

"Never do anything when you are in a temper, for you will do everything wrong."

Baltasar Gracián (1601–1658)

"Never speak when you are angry. If you do you'll make the best speech you'll ever regret."

> *Robert Lynd (1879–1949), as quoted by G. F. Lamb in* Harrap's Book of Humorous Quotations, *1990*

"Never lose [your] temper till it would be detrimental to keep it."

> *Sean O'Casey (1884–1964), The Plough and the Stars, 1926*

ANIMALS

"Never send a man to do a horse's job."

> *Mr. Ed, in "Mr. Ed"*

"Never try to teach a pig to sing; it's a waste of time, and it annoys the pig."

> *Anonymous, variously attributed*

"Never wrestle with a pig. You get dirty, and besides, the pig likes it."

Cyrus Ching (1876–1967)

APOLOGIES

"Never make a defense or an apology until you are accused."

> *Charles I (1600–1649) of England, who, after being accused, was tried and beheaded*

"Never apologize and never explain—it's a sign of weakness."

> *John Wayne (1907–1979), in* She Wore a Yellow Ribbon, *1949*

"Never . . . apologize. The right sort of people do not want apologies, and the wrong sort take a mean advantage of them."

> *P. G. Wodehouse (1881–1975)*

APPLAUSE

"Never quite believe it."

Robert Montgomery (1904–1981)

ARGUING

"Never argue with an idiot—folks might not be able to tell the difference."

Anonymous

"Never get in a battle of wits without any ammunition."

Anonymous

"Never maintain an argument with heat and clamour, though you think or know yourself to be in the right; but give your opinions modestly and coolly, which is the only way to convince. . . ."

> *Earl of Chesterfield (1694–1773), in a letter to his son, October 16, 1747*

"Never ever pick a fight,
    'Cause it never ever proves who's right."

> *Howdy Doody, in "The Howdy Doody Show"*

"Never contend with a man who has nothing to lose."

> *Baltasar Gracián (1601–1658), The Art of Worldly Wisdom*

"Never call anybody an asshole. It hardly ever works."

> *Marilyn Peterson, as quoted by Merrit Malloy and Shauna Sorensen in* The Quotable Quote Book, *1972*

"Never argue at the dinner table, for the one who is not hungry always gets the best of the argument."

> *Archbishop Richard Whately (1787–1863), English theologian*

ART AND ARTISTS

"Never put more than two waves in a picture; it's fussy."

> *Winslow Homer (1836–1910), as quoted by Lloyd Goodrich,* Winslow Homer

"Never forget that art is not a form of propaganda; it is a form of truth."

John F. Kennedy (1917–1963)

AUTOMOBILES

"Never drive with a doctor or a nun. Doctors are lost in dreams of Medicaid Heaven and average 17 miles an hour on the open highway. Nuns are dreaming of the conventional heaven, and because they are all presumably in a state of grace, they go 92 miles an hour on city streets."

Anonymous contributor, as quoted by Ann Landers

"Never lend your car to anyone to whom you have given birth."

Erma Bombeck (1927–   )

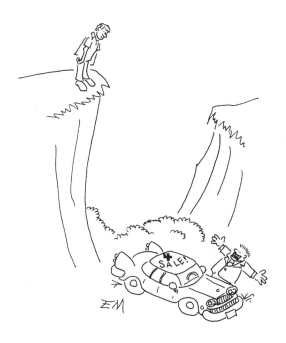

"Never buy a car that's being sold at the bottom of a ravine."

Joey Adams (1911–   )

"Never get your flat tire fixed by a guy who's chewing gum."

Johnny Hart (1931–), in his comic strip "B.C."

BARS

"Never argue with the bouncer. . . . Never argue with a regular customer—the bouncer always decides in his favor."

Ken Cruickshank, columnist, the Florida-Times Union, Jacksonville, June 25, 1978

"Never put your money in a bank where the bank president's portrait is a mug shot."

> *Johnny Hart (1931–   ),*
> *in his comic strip "B.C."*

BEAUTY

"Never lose an opportunity of seeing anything that is beautiful; for beauty is God's handwriting—a wayside sacrament."

Ralph Waldo Emerson (1803–1882)

"Never [is it that beauty] lasts in this world. God and man and large dogs see to that."

Kinky Friedman, Greenwich Killing Time

BEGINNINGS

"Never start anything important on Friday."

Anonymous

"Never order a drink where you get to keep the glass."

> *Paul Dickson (1939–   ), quoting Roger Simon in* The New Official Rules, *1989*

"Never start something you don't want to finish."

American adage

"Never start off on the wrong foot."

Anonymous

BELIEF

"Never believe on faith, see for yourself!"

*Bertolt Brecht (1898–1956),
playwright,* The Mother

"Never believe in mirrors or newspapers."

*John Osborne (1929–   ), British
playwright,* The Hotel in Amsterdam,
1968

BOASTING

"Never crow till you're out of the woods."

American adage

BOOKS

"Never judge a book by its cover."

English adage

"Never judge a book by its movie."

J. W. Eagan (1925–1987)

"The three practical rules, then, which I have to offer, are (1) Never read any book that is not a year old. (2) Never read any but famed books. (3) Never read any but what you like."

Ralph Waldo Emerson (1803–1882), "Books," Society and Solitude, 1870

"Never lend books, for no one ever returns them; the only books I have in my library are books that other folks have lent me."

Anatole France (Jacques-Anatole-François Thibault) (1844–1924), La Vie Littéraire, 1888–1892

"Never trust the teller. Trust the tale."

D. H. Lawrence (1885–1930), Studies in Classic American Literature

"Never read a book before reviewing it—it prejudices a man so!"

> *Sydney Smith (1771–1845), as quoted in* The Smith of Smiths, *1934, by H. Pearson*

"Never disregard a book because the author of it is a foolish fellow."

> *Viscount Melbourne [William Lamb] (1779–1848), as quoted by John Gross in* The Oxford Book of Aphorisms, *1983*

"Never go anywhere without a cheap book or magazine to read."

> *Bill Moyers (1934–   ), quoting a mentor,* TV Guide, *August 13, 1994*

"Never read a book if it were possible to talk for half an hour with the man who wrote it."

> *Woodrow Wilson (1856–1924), in a speech at Princeton University, 1910*

"Never read a book through merely because you have begun it."

> *John Witherspoon (1723–1794)*

BRIBERY

"Never underestimate the effectiveness of a straight cash bribe."

> *Claude Cockburn (1904–1981), The Village Voice, October 4, 1976*

BUREAUCRATS

"Never say without qualification that your
activity has sufficient space, money, staff,
etc."

> *Douglas Evelyn, of the National
> Portrait Gallery, Washington, D.C.,
> advising other bureaucrats*

BUSINESS

"Never forget one little point. It's my
business. You just work here."

> *Elizabeth Arden (1884–1966),
> cosmetics tycoon, speaking to her
> husband, as quoted by Alfred Lewis
> and Constance Woodworth in* Miss
> Elizabeth Arden, *1972*

"Never trust anyone who puts your prosperity above their own."

Ferengi adage, "Deep Space Nine"

"Never sell the sheep's hide when you can sell the wool."

German adage

"Never have partners."

The father of Howard Hughes, as quoted by Donald L. Bartlett and James B. Steele in Empire, *1979*

"Never invest your money in anything that eats or needs repainting."

Billy Rose (1899–1966), theatrical producer, New York Post, *October 26, 1957*

"Never have sex with the boss's sister."

Ferengi adage, "Deep Space Nine"

BUSYBODIES

"Never thrust your own sickle into
   another's corn."

> *Publilius Syrus (first century B.C.)*

CATS

"Never try to use a cat's claw for a
   toothpick."

> *Randy Glasbergen, as Stanley Parker
> in Glasbergen's comic strip "The
> Better Half"*

"Never try to outstubborn a cat."

> *Lazarus Long, a book character
> created by Robert A. Heinlein
> (1907–1988),* Time Enough for Love:
> The Further Adventures of Lazarus
> Long, *1973*

CAUTION

"Never test the depth of a river with both feet."

African adage

"Never go rattlesnake hunting in earmuffs."

Anonymous

"Never laugh at live dragons."

Bilbo Baggins, a book character created by J. R. R. Tolkien (1892–1973)

"Never kick a mule and turn your back."

American adage

"Never cast an anchor in shifting sands."

American adage

"Never engage in a winter sport with an ambulance parked at the bottom of the hill."

> *Erma Bombeck (1927–   ),*
> *columnist, as quoted in* The Last Word
> *by Carolyn Warner, 1992*

"Never let those ruby slippers off your feet for a moment, or you'll be at the mercy of the Wicked Witch of the West."

> *Billie Burke (1885–1970), as Glinda,*
> *the Good Witch of the North, to Judy*
> *Garland as Dorothy in* The Wizard of
> Oz *(1939)*

Never Cross a Vampire

> *Title of a book by Stuart Kaminsky,*
> *1995*

"Never turn your back."

> *Nikita S. Khrushchev (1894–1971)*

"Never play leapfrog with a unicorn."

American adage

"Never drop your gun to hug a bear."

H. E. Palmer, A Fable, 1946

"Never stand between a dog and the hydrant."

*John Peers, quoting "Cliff's Law,"
1,001 Logical Laws, 1979*

"Never leave hold of what you've got until you've got hold of something else."

*Barnstormers' adage, as quoted by
Donald Herzberg (1925–1980), dean of
Georgetown University's graduate
school*

"Never insult an alligator until after you have crossed the river."

*Cordell Hull (1872–1955), 1945 Nobel
Peace Prize winner*

"Never stow away on a Kamikaze plane."

Paul Dickson (1939–   ), quoting T. R. M. Spence in The New Official Rules, *1989*

"Never trouble trouble till trouble troubles you."

> *Anonymous, favorite saying of John Joseph Powers (1876–1954)*

"Never step in anything soft."

> *John Peers, quoting "Pulliam's Postulate," 1,001 Logical Laws, 1979*

"Never take the antidote before the poison."

> *Roman adage*

"Never lose your cigar cutter in your pocket."

> *Martha Stewart (1941–   ), "Late Show with David Letterman," January 1995*

"Never kick a fresh turd on a hot day."

> *Harry S Truman (1884–1972)*

"Never too late to mend."

> *Anonymous optimist (seventeenth century)*

"Never wait for trouble."

> *Chuck Yeager (1923–   ), test pilot,*
> *the first man to fly faster than the*
> *speed of sound*

CHARACTER

"Never does a person describe his own
character more clearly than by his way of
describing that of others."

> *Jean Paul Friedrich Richter*
> *(1763–1825)*

"Never teach false morality. How exqui-
sitely absurd to teach a girl that beauty is
of no value, dress of no use! . . . The great
thing is to teach her their just value, and
that there must be something better under
the bonnet than a pretty face, for real
happiness. But never sacrifice truth."

> *Sydney Smith (1771–1845)*

CHILDREN

"Never reprimand a boy in the evening—
darkness and a troubled mind are a poor
combination."

> *Frank Boyden,* Life, November 1962

"Never hire a baby-sitter with more tattoos
than Guns 'N Roses."

> *Brett Butler (1958–   ), as Grace
> Kelly in "Grace Under Fire"*

"Never say 'that was before your time,'
because the last full moon was before their
time."

> *Bill Cosby (1937–   ) on children*

"Never sound sarcastic when you give
praise."

> Ladies Home Journal

"Never have ideas about children—and never have ideas *for* them."

> D. H. Lawrence (1885–1930), Fantasia of the Unconscious, 1922

"Never allow your child to call you by your first name. He hasn't known you long enough."

> *Fran Lebowitz (1950–   ),* Social Studies, 1981

"Never let your children think you have favorites."

> *Suzanne Braun Levine (1941–   ), editor*

"Never change diapers in midstream."

> *Don Marquis (1878–1937), humorist*

"Never raise your hand to your children—it leaves your midsection unprotected."

Robert Orben (1927–   ), humorist

"Never leave children alone in a car. They seem to know almost instinctively how to release the emergency brake."

Reader's Digest, Household Hints & Handy Tips, *1988*

"Never play peekaboo with a child on a long plane trip. There's no end to the game. Finally I grabbed him by the bib and said, 'Look, it's always gonna be me!'"

Rita Rudner (1955–   )

"Never fret for an only son, the idea of failure will never occur to him."

George Bernard Shaw (1856–1950), as quoted by Alistair Cooke, America, *1973*

"Never have children; only have
grandchildren."

> *Gore Vidal (1925–   )*

CHOICE

"Never choose between two good things;
take both."

> *American adage*

CLOTHING

Never Buy a Hat If Your Feet Are Cold

> *Title of a book by Ken Felderstein,
> 1990*

Never Heave Your Bosom in a Front Hook Bra

> *Title of a book by Modine Gunch, 1992*

"Never try to wear a hat that has more
character than you do."

Lance Morrow (1939–   ), essayist

"Never darken my Dior again!"

> *Beatrice Lillie (Lady Peel)*
> *(1898–1989), comic actress, to a*
> *waiter at a Buckingham Palace dinner*
> *after he spilled soup on her gown*

"Never buy a fur from a veterinarian."

> *Joan Rivers (1937–   )*

"Never wear red, or you'll be taken for a hussy."

> *Anonymous mother, as quoted by*
> *Michele Slung in More Momilies, 1986*

"Never, ever, wear red."

> *Trekker adage, derived from the short*
> *life spans of characters who wore*
> *crimson security uniforms on "Star*
> *Trek"*

"Never wear polyester underwear if you're going to be hit by lightning."

> *Marsha Warfield (1954–   ), as Roz in "Night Court"*

COMPLAINING

"Never complain and never explain."

> *Benjamin Disraeli (1804–1881), as quoted in* The Life of William Ewart Gladstone *by John Morley, 1968*

"Never complain. Complaints will always discredit you. Rather than compassion, they provoke insolence and encourage others to behave like those we complain about. It is better to praise others, so as to win still more favors of them."

> *Baltasar Gracián (1601–1658)*

CONCEIT

"Never [have] any pity for conceited
people, because I think they carry their
comfort about with them."

> *George Eliot (Marian Evans)*
> *(1819–1880),* The Mill on the Floss,
> *1860*

CONCENTRATION

"Never let the clowns run away with the
circus."

> *American adage*

"Never do anything you wouldn't want to see published in your hometown paper."

Anonymous mother, as quoted by Michele Slung in More Momilies, *1986*

CONDUCT

"Never tell a lie, nor take what is not your own, nor sue for slander. *Settle them cases yourself.*"

> *Elizabeth Hutchinson Jackson, the mother of Andrew Jackson (17??–1791), giving her last advice to her son, who would become president*

"Never take sides in anything. Taking sides is the beginning of sincerity, and earnestness follows shortly afterward, and the human being becomes a bore."

> *Oscar Wilde (1854–1900)*

CONSCIENCE

"Never do anything against conscience,
even if the state demands it."

Albert Einstein (1879–1955)

"Never undertake anything for which you
wouldn't have the courage to ask the
blessings of Heaven."

*Georg Christoph Lichtenbergh
(1742–1799)*

"Never . . . do wrong when people are
looking."

*Mark Twain (Samuel Clemens)
(1835–1910)*

"Never do anything that one cannot talk
about after dinner."

*Oscar Wilde (1854–1900), explaining
why one shouldn't commit murder*

CONSUMER ADVICE

"Never decide to buy something while
listening to the salesman."

> *Edmund C. Berkeley, "Right Answers—
> A Short Guide for Obtaining Them,"*
> Computers and Automation,
> *September 1969*

"Never pay for work before it's completed."

> *H. Jackson Brown, Jr.*

"Never shop in a place that has 'bargain' in
its name."

> *Ken Cruickshank, columnist, the*
> Florida Times-Union, *Jacksonville,*
> *June 25, 1978*

"Never buy what you do not want, because it is cheap; it will be dear to you."

> *Thomas Jefferson (1743–1826), A Decalogue of canons for observation in practical life, in a letter to Thomas Jefferson Smith, February 21, 1825*

"Never buy a thing you don't want merely because it is dear."

> *Oscar Wilde (1854–1900)*

"Never buy a hand tool that does not have the manufacturer's name permanently inscribed on it. The absence of a name indicates poor quality."

> *Dirck Z. Meengs, as quoted by Tom Parker in* Rules of Thumb 2, 1987

"Never do business with anybody who knocks at your door offering to repave your driveway, replace your windows, waterproof your basement, tune your furnace, or repair your roof."

William Young, director of consumer affairs for the National Association of Home Builders

COURAGE

"Never expect to steal third base while keeping one foot on second."

Anonymous

"Never befriend the oppressed unless you are prepared to take on the oppressor."

Ogden Nash (1902–1971)

CRIME

"Never sleep with a suspect."

> *Gene Barry as Amos Burke in "Burke's Law"*

"Never ask when you can take."

> *Ferengi adage, "Deep Space Nine"*

"Never try to buy a man too cheap."

> *Archie Goodwin, assistant to detective Nero Wolfe, stating one of the rules of being an organized crime boss in* In the Best Families *by Rex Stout (1886–1975), 1950*

"Never steal anything small."

> *Crooks' adage. Amended by P. J.*
> *O'Rourke (1947–) to: "Never steal*
> *anything so small that you'll have to go*
> *to an unpleasant city jail for it instead*
> *of a minimum-security federal tennis*
> *prison."*

"Never steal more than you actually need,
for the possession of surplus money leads
to extravagance, foppish attire, frivolous
thought."

> *Dalton Trumbo (1906–1976),*
> *screenwriter*

"Never get deeply in debt to someone who
cried at the end of *Scarface*."

> *Robert S. Wieder (1944–), San*
> Francisco Chronicle, *June 5, 1986*

CRITICS AND CRITICIZING

"Never criticize a man until you've walked a mile in his moccasins."

> *Native American adage*

"Never confuse the audience with the critics."

> *Robert Preston (1918–1987), as a playwright in* Rehearsal for Murder, *1982*

DARKNESS

"Never fear shadows. They simply mean there's a light shining somewhere nearby."

> *Ruth E. Renkel,* Reader's Digest, *1983*

DATING

"Never date a man who wears more jewelry—or worries more about his wardrobe—than you."

> *Lara Flynn Boyle (1970–   ),*
> *quoting her mother, 1994*

"Never try to pick up a woman who is wearing a Super Bowl ring."

> *Garry Shandling (1949–   ), as*
> *quoted by Paul Dickson (1939–   )*
> *in* The New Official Rules, *1989*

"Never date a woman whose father calls her 'Princess.' Chances are she believes it."

> *Wes Smith (1930–   )*

EM

"Never date a man whose belt buckle is
bigger than his head."

*Brett Butler, as Grace Kelly in "Grace
Under Fire"*

61

DEATH

"Never speak ill of the dead."

Old English adage

"Never does one feel oneself so utterly helpless as in trying to speak comfort for great bereavement."

Jane Welsh Carlyle (1801–1866), letter to Thomas Carlyle, December 27, 1853

"Never send to know for whom the bell tolls; it tolls for thee."

John Donne (1573–1631), Devotions, 1624

DEBT

"Never run into debt, not if you can find anything else to run into."

Josh Billings (Henry Wheeler Shaw) (1818–1885), humorist, The Complete Works of Josh Billings, *1919*

DENTISTS

"Never set foot into a dentist's surgery without checking into the psychological well-being of the man with the drill in his hand."

Inspector Maigret, a character created by Georges Simenon (1903–1989), in "Mystery!"

DESPAIR

"Never despair."

> *Horace (Quintus Horatius Flaccus)*
> *(65–8 B.C.)*

"Never must we despair, never must we give in, but we must face facts and draw true conclusions from them."

> *Winston Churchill (1874–1965),*
> *during the dark days of World War II*

"Never despair, but if you do, work on in despair."

> *Edmund Burke (1729–1797)*

"Never give way to melancholy; resist it steadily, for the habit will encroach."

> *Sydney Smith (1771–1845), Lady*
> Holland's Memoir, *1855*

DIPLOMACY

"Never lie, but never tell the entire truth either."

> *Anonymous diplomat, British Foreign Service*

"Never negotiate out of fear . . . never fear to negotiate."

> *John F. Kennedy (1917–1963), inaugural address, January 20, 1961*

DOCTORS

"Never trust a doctor who sells cemetery plots on the side."

> *Anonymous*

"Never accept a drink from a urologist."

> *Erma Bombeck (1927–   ), quoting her father, as quoted by Anthony Brown in an article for the* Los Angeles Times *syndicate*

"Never go to a doctor whose office plants have died."

> *Erma Bombeck (1927–   )*

"Never argue with a doctor; he has inside information."

> *Bob Elliott (1923–   ) and Ray Goulding (1922–1990)*

Dogs

"Never have a dog. Let's not beat around the bush here: dogs are morons. . . . We have always had dogs, and they have faithfully performed many valuable services for us, such as: 1. Peeing on everything. 2. When we're driving in our car, alerting us that we have passed another dog by barking real loud in our ears for the next 114 miles. 3. Trying to kill the Avon lady."

Dave Barry (1947–   ), Homes and Other Black Holes, 1988

"Never visit people who own a poodle. If you do visit people who own a poodle, never throw a ball or small squeak toy to the poodle if you wish to be left alone during the remainder of the visit."

Paul Dickson (1939–   ), quoting John H. Corcoran, Jr., in The Official Explanation, 1950

"Never yell fireplug in a crowded kennel."

Mike Peters (1943–   ), as Grimm,
in his comic strip "Mother Goose and
Grimm," January 1994

Never Trust a Calm Dog

Title of a book by Tom Parker, 1990

"Never ignore the barking of wise old dogs.
According to a Norwegian proverb, when
the old dog barks, you'd better look out
the window."

Elizabeth Marshall Thomas
(1932–   ), author of The Hidden
Life of Dogs, *1994*

DREAMS

"Never listen to anybody else, no matter how clever or expert they may appear. Keep your eyes open and your ears shut, and as the Americans say—'*Go for it.*'"

> *Michael Caine (1933–), What's It All About?, 1992*

DRUGS

"Never smoke opium, my boy. Terribly constipating stuff—consider the wretched poet Coleridge. Green about the gills and a stranger to the lavatory."

> *John Mortimer (1923–), writer, quoting his father Clifford Mortimer,* The New Yorker, March 6, 1995

EDUCATION

"Never teach your child to be cunning, for you may be certain you will be one of the very first victims of his shrewdness."

Josh Billings (Henry Wheeler Shaw) (1818–1885)

"Never learn to do anything: if you don't learn, you'll always find someone else who'll do it for you."

Jane Clemens, mother of Samuel Clemens (Mark Twain) (1835–1910)

"Never let your schooling interfere with your education."

Mark Twain (Samuel Clemens) (1835–1910)

EFFORT

"Never do anything standing that you can do sitting, or anything sitting that you can do lying down."

Chinese adage

"Never do anything yourself that you can get someone else to do."

Anonymous sluggard

"Never stop, never weary, and never give in."

Winston Churchill (1874–1965)

"Never, never, let the flame go out."

Winston Churchill (1874–1965), speaking of how to smoke a cigar; however, the advice applies to other more important activities as well

"Never confuse motion with action."

Ernest Hemingway (1899–1961), as quoted by Marlene Dietrich in A. E. Hotchner, Papa Hemingway, *1966*

"Never give up and never give in."

Hubert Humphrey (1911–1978)

Egotists

"Never underestimate a man who overestimates himself."

Franklin D. Roosevelt (1882–1945), describing Gen. Douglas MacArthur

EMOTION

"Never apologize for showing feeling. When you do so, you apologize for truth."

Benjamin Disraeli (1804–1881)

"Never be ashamed to say what you feel. And if you come to love a man, let him know it. Let him know all about it."

Robert Preston (1918–1987), to Shirley Knight, playing his daughter, in The Dark at the Top of the Stairs *(1960)*

"Never feel guilty about having warm human feelings toward anyone."

Lorne Greene (1915–1987), as Ben Cartwright, talking heart-to-heart with Little Joe in "Bonanza"

ENDINGS

"Never think you've seen the last of anything."

> *Eudora Welty (1909–   ), The Optimist's Daughter, 1968*

ENEMIES

"Never ascribe to an opponent motives meaner than your own."

> *James M. Barrie (1860–1937), Scottish dramatist and novelist, rectorial address, St. Andrews, May 3, 1922*

"Never hold a grudge against an enemy for long. . . . Always trash him quickly while what he did to you is fresh in your mind."

Christopher Kelly Brown (1952–   ), as Hagar in his comic strip "Hagar the Horrible," April 1, 1993

"Never interrupt an enemy while he's making a mistake."

Napoleon Bonaparte (1769–1821)

"Never tell thy foe that thy foot acheth."

Old English adage, dating to at least the early fourteenth century

"Never maltreat the enemy by halves."

Winston Churchill (1874–1965)

ENTERTAINING

"Never use scented candles—they can have an unappetizing effect."

> *Craig Claiborne (1920–   ), food expert*

"Never give a party if you will be the most interesting person there."

> *Mickey Friedman (1944–   ), mystery writer*

EVIL

"Never open the door to a lesser evil, for other and greater ones invariably slink in after it."

> *Baltasar Gracián (1601–1658)*

"Never do evil for the sake of good."

> *Italian adage (common to other cultures as well)*

"Never make friends with the devil, brother; his pitchfork will get you in the end."

> *Ross Martin (1929–1981), as Artemus Gordon in "The Wild, Wild West"*

"Never label a necessary evil as good."

> *Margaret Mead (1901–1978),* Redbook, *November 1978*

"Never wonder to see men wicked. . . . wonder to see them not ashamed."

> *Jonathan Swift (1667–1745), satiric author and cleric,* Thoughts on Various Subjects, *1711*

EXAGGERATION

"Never exaggerate. Superlatives offend the
truth and cast doubt on your judgment.
The prudent show restraint, and would
rather fall short than long. To overvalue
something is a form of lying. It can ruin
your reputation for good taste and
wisdom."

> *Baltasar Gracián (1601–1658)*

"Never serve a rabbit stew before you catch
the rabbit."

> *James Thurber (1894–1961),* Further
> Fables for Our Time

EXPENSES

"Never let your expenditures drop too low
or people will start to question your
conceptual package."

> *Stanley Bing, giving a cautionary rule
> for success in Hollywood,* Esquire,
> *March 1993*

EXPLANATIONS

"Never retreat. Never explain. Get it done
and let them howl."

> *Benjamin Jowett (1817–1893),
> classicist and lecturer*

"Never explain. Your friends do not need it, and your enemies will not believe you anyway."

> *Elbert Hubbard (1856–1915),* The Note Book of Elbert Hubbard, *1927*

"Never give any reasons. Your decisions may be right, but your reasons are sure to be wrong."

> *Lord Mansfield (1705–1793)*

FAILURE

"Never confuse a single defeat with a final defeat."

> *F. Scott Fitzgerald (1896–1940)*

"Never give a man up until he has failed at something he likes."

Lewis E. Lawes, warden of Sing Sing prison, quoted in Little Gazette, *October 1969*

FALSEHOOD

"Never . . . think you can turn over any old falsehood without a terrible squirming of the horrid little population that dwells under it."

Oliver Wendell Holmes (1809–1894)

FAMILY

"Never let anyone outside the family know what you're thinking."

> *Marlon Brando (1924–   ), as Don Corleone, in* The Godfather, *1972*

"Never allow family to stand in the way of opportunity."

> *Ferengi adage, "Deep Space Nine"*

Never Trust a Sister Over Twelve

> *Title of a book by Stephen Roos, 1993*

FASHION

"Never despise fashion. It's what we have instead of God."

> *Malcolm Bradbury (1932–), academic and critic, as quoted in* In & Out: Debrett 1980–81 *by Neil Mackwood*

"Never fashionable . . . never unfashionable."

> *Harrison Ford (1942–)*

"Never confuse elegance with snobbery."

> *Yves Saint Laurent (1936–), French couturier,* Rita, 1984

FAVORS

"Never claim as a right what you can ask as a favor."

> *John Churton Collins (1848–1908)*

"Never let your inferiors do you a favor. It will be extremely costly."

> *H. L. Mencken (1880–1956),*
> *"Sententiae," The Vintage Mencken,*
> *1955*

"Never run after your hat—others will be delighted to do it; why spoil their fun."

> *Mark Twain (Samuel Clemens)*
> *(1835–1910)*

"Never show your teeth unless you're
prepared to bite."

French adage

FIGHTING

"Never hit a man with glasses. Hit him
with something bigger and heavier."

Anonymous

"Never strike a king unless you are sure
you shall kill him."

Ralph Waldo Emerson (1803–1882)

"Never fight fair with a stranger, boy. You'll
never get out of the jungle that way."

Ben Loman, in Death of a Salesman,
1947, by Arthur Miller (1915–   )

"Never shoot blanks."

*Richard Nixon (1913–1994), Look,
October 19, 1971*

"Never insult seven men if you're only carrying a six-shooter."

Harry Morgan, as Col. Sherman Potter in "M*A*S*H"

"Never draw your dirk when a blow will
do it."

> *Scots adage*

"Never take a punch at a man named
'Sullivan.'"

> *H. Allen Smith (1907–1976), humorist
> and journalist,* Life in a Putty Knife
> Factory

FIRST

"Never be first to do anything."

> *Ken S. of Wayland, Massachusetts, as
> quoted by Ann Landers, 1978*

FOOD

"Never ask what goes into a hot dog."

American adage

Never Eat Anything Bigger than Your Head

Title of a book by B. Kliban (d. 1990), 1976

"Never eat anything whose listed ingredients cover more than one-third of the package."

Joseph Leonard, as quoted by Herb Caen in the San Francisco Chronicle, *March 3, 1986*

Never Let a Skinny Guy Make Sandwiches

Title of a book by Gene Mueller and Bob Denyer, 1994

"Never be ashamed to eat your meat."

> *Old English adage, dating to at least 1639*

"Never eat more in a single day than your head weighs."

> *Jim Harrison (1937–   ), food writer and novelist*

"Never cut an oyster. It makes the thing look even worse. . . . Never drink iced tea with a meal anywhere but in Indiana."

> *John Mariani*, Esquire, March 1993

"Never eat more than you can lift."

> *Miss Piggy (1958?–   ), Miss Piggy's Guide to Life (As Told to Henry Beard), 1981*

"Never begin a business negotiation on an empty stomach."

> *Quark, quoting the third Ferengi Rule of Acquisition, "Deep Space Nine"*

"Never eat prunes when you're hungry."

> *John Peers, quoting "Schmidt's Law," 1,001 Logical Laws, 1979*

"Never eat tuna fish at a drugstore."

> *Anonymous mother, as quoted by Michele Slung in More Momilies, 1986*

FOOLS

"Never call a man a fool; borrow from him."

> *Addison Mizner (1872–1933), architect*

FORGIVENESS

"Never does the human soul appear so
strong as when it forgoes revenge, and
dares forgive an injury."

E. H. Chapin (1814–1880)

"Never forget, rarely forgive."

*Edward I. Koch (1924–   ), former
mayor of New York City*

FRIENDS

"Never trample on the people you
encounter on the way up; you'll see them
again on the way down."

American adage

"Never have a companion who casts you in the shade."

> Baltasar Gracián (1601–1658)

"Never try to be nice to a man with a tattoo on his face."

> Paul Dickson (1939–   ), The Official Explanation, 1980

"Never apologize for your terrible friends. We are all *somebody's* terrible friends."

> Jack Gallagher, as quoted by Bernard Levin in his column, London Times, July 9, 1980

"Never speak ill of yourself; your friends will always say enough on that subject."

> Charles-Maurice de Talleyrand-Périgord (1754–1838), French statesman, as quoted by J. R. Solly, A Cynic's Breviary, 1925

FUTILITY

"Never comb a bald head."

Old English adage

FUTURE, THE

"Never let the future disturb you. You will meet it, if you have to, with the same weapons of reason which today arm you against the present."

Marcus Aurelius Antoninus (121–180), Roman emperor

"Never think of the future. It comes soon enough."

Albert Einstein (1879–1955)

GAMBLING

"Never bet on baseball."

Pete Rose (1941–   )

GENTLEMAN, ENGLISH

"I trust you know the 'Three Nevers for Proper Gentlemen'?
Never shoot south of the Thames—
Never follow whisky with port—
Never have your wife in the morning—
The day may have something better to offer—"

P. V. Taylor

GENTLENESS

"Never touch a butterfly's wing with your finger."

> *Colette (1873–1954)*

"Never cut what you can untie."

> *Joseph Joubert (1754–1824)*

GIFTS

Never Sniff a Gift Fish

> *Title of a book by Patrick McManus, 1983*

"Never look a gift horse in the mouth."

> *St. Jerome,* On the Epistle to the Ephesians *(c. A.D. 420)*

"Never hate a man enough to give him his diamonds back."

Zsa Zsa Gabor (1918?–   )

"Never . . . give a man a present when he's feeling good. You want to do it when he's down."

Lyndon B. Johnson (1908–1973), as quoted by Doris Kearns Goodwin in Lyndon B. Johnson and the Amazing Dream

GOD

"Never invoke gods unless you really want them to appear. It annoys them very much."

G. K. Chesterton (1874–1936)

"Never . . . say that you are alone, for you are not alone; nay, God is within, and your genius is within. And what need have they of light to see what you are doing?"

Epictetus (c. 50–120)

"Never practice your newfound assertiveness training skills on the God of Abraham, Isaac, and Jacob!"

Doug Marlette (1949–   ), as Rev. Will B. Dunn, after making too many demands in a prayer and being blasted by a thunderbolt in Marlette's comic strip "Kudzu"

"Never forget that [God] tests his real friends more severely than the lukewarm ones."

Kathryn Hulme (1900–1981), The Nun's Story, *1956*

GOLF

"Never stand too close to the ball after you hit it."

> *Herbert V. Prochnow (1897–   ) and*
> *Herbert V. Prochnow, Jr. (1931–   ),*
> The Toastmaster's Treasure Chest,
> *1979*

GOOD-BYES

"Never part without loving words to think of during your absence. It may be that you will not meet again in life."

> *Jean Paul Friedrich Richter*
> *(1763–1825)*

"Never say 'good-bye.'"

> *Groucho Marx (1890–1977), who*
> *despised departures*

GOODNESS

"Never be weary of well doing."

> *English adage, cited in Thomas Draxe's* Bibliotheca Scholastica Instructissima, *1633*

"Never . . . be mean in anything; never be false; never be cruel."

> *Charles Dickens (1812–1870),* David Copperfield, *1849–1850*

"Never appeal to a man's 'better nature'—he might not have one."

> *Robert A. Heinlein (1907–1988)*

GOSSIP

"Never gossip about people you don't know. This deprives simple artisans like Truman Capote of work."

> *P. J. O'Rourke (1947–   ), Modern Manners, 1983*

"Never use the word *gossip* in a pejorative sense. It's the stuff of biography and has to be woven in."

> *Joan Peyser (1931–   ), musicologist and writer, Publishers Weekly, 1987*

"Never believe anything bad about anybody unless you positively know it to be true; never tell even that unless you feel that it is absolutely necessary—and remember that God is listening while you tell it."

> *Henry Van Dyke (1852–1933), as quoted by Edythe Draper in Quotations for the Christian World, 1981*

GUNS

"Never run away from a gun. Bullets can travel faster than you can."

Wild Bill Hickock (1837–1876)

HAPPINESS

"Never lose your sense of humor. The happiest people are the ones who are able to laugh at themselves."

Sarah Delany and A. Elizabeth Delany (both in their 100s), with Amy Hill Hearth, The Delany Sisters' Book of Everyday Wisdom, *1994*

"Never mind your happiness; do your duty."

Will Durant (1885–1981), historian

"Never miss an opportunity to make others happy even if you have to leave them alone to do it."

Anonymous

HASTE

"Never hurry and never worry!"

E. B. White (1899–1985), Charlotte's advice to Wilbur, Charlotte's Web, *1952*

HATE

"*Never let yourself* hate *any person. It is the most devastating weapon of one's enemies.*"

> *Dr. Thomas Norval Hepburn, in a letter to his daughter Katharine Hepburn, as quoted in her book* Me, *1991*

"Never get discouraged, never be petty; always remember, others may hate you. Those who hate you don't win unless you hate them. And then you destroy yourself."

> *Richard Nixon (1913–1994), in his farewell address to his staff, August 9, 1974*

HEALTH

"Never let your mind write a check your body can't cash."

> *Lewis Grizzard (1946–1994)*, Chili Dawgs Always Bark at Night, *1989*

"Never get fat, dear child. Fat smothers anyone's vitality."

> *Margot Asquith (1864–1945), Scottish-born British political figure, to Anita Loos, quoted in* Kiss Hollywood Good-Bye

"Never floss with a stranger."

> *Joan Rivers (1937–   )*

HOLLYWOOD

"Never buy anything you can't put on the *Chief*."

> *Movie actor's adage, 1930s. The Chief was the train out of town. Clark Gable often used this phrase when he was first in Hollywood.*

HOPE

"Never quit certainty for hope."

> *English adage*

"Never look on the bright side; the glare is blinding."

> *Florence King (1936–   ), author,*
> National Review, *December 31, 1994*

"Never let the things we can't have, or don't have, or shouldn't have, spoil our enjoyment of the things we do have and can have. As we value our happiness let us not forget it, for one of the greatest lessons in life is learning to be happy without the things we cannot or should not have."

Richard L. Evans (1906–1971),
journalist

HOUSEWORK

"Never learn how to iron a man's shirt or you'll wind up having to do it."

Anonymous mother, as quoted by
Michele Slung in Momilies, *1985*

HUMOR

"Never take a Puritan to the 'Monty Python' show."

Professor Richard Shweder, Department of Psychology, University of Chicago, November 1993

"Never joke in the presence of a prince. He may miss the punch line and take your laughter personally."

Anonymous

"Never, never try to be funny! The actors must be serious. Only the situation must be absurd. Funny is in the writing, not in the performing. If the situation isn't absurd, no amount of hoke will help."

Mel Brooks (1926–   )

"Never make people laugh. If you would succeed in life, you must be solemn, solemn as an ass. All the great monuments are built over solemn asses."

Senator Thomas Corwin (1794–1865), to James Garfield, who went on to become U.S. president

"The three cardinal rules for comics:
1. Never follow a better comic.
2. Never give a heckler the last word.
3. Never let them see you sweat."

Brian Haley

"Never grind your ax."

Leslie Nielsen (1922–   ), giving one of the rules of movie comedy

INDEPENDENCE

"Never for a day let them forget that you
can pick up your marbles and go home."

> *Douglas Dillon (1909–   )*

"Never depend on anyone except yourself."

> *Jean de La Fontaine (1621–1695),*
> Fables

INHERITANCE

"Never say you know a man until you have
divided an inheritance with him."

> *Johann Kaspar Lavater (1741–1801),*
> *Swiss poet and philosopher,* Aphorisms
> on Man, *c. 1788*

INSULTS

"Never tell anybody to go to hell unless
you can make them go."

> *Lyndon Baines Johnson (1908–1973),*
> *quoting the best lesson he had been*
> *taught by Sam Rayburn (1882–1961)*

INTELLIGENCE

"Never be clever but when you cannot
help it."

> *Richard Fulke Greville (1544–1628),*
> *Maxims, Characters and Reflections,*
> *1756*

INTUITION

"Never use intuition."

> Omar N. Bradley (1893–1981), U.S.
> general during World War II

INVITATIONS

"Never accept an invitation from a stranger
unless he offers you candy."

> Linda Festa

JOB INTERVIEWING

"Never wear a backwards baseball cap to
an interview unless applying for the job of
umpire. . . . Just as important as what you
say during an interview is what your body
is saying about you, so be sure to conceal
any tattoos that say: 'Work sucks, let's
party.'"

Dan Zevin, Entry-Level Life, *1994*

JUDGMENT

"Never judge a man by the words of his
mother; listen to the words of his
neighbors."

Yiddish adage

"Never judge before you see."

Anonymous

"Never judge a horse by its harness."

Country adage

JUSTICE

"Never forget that the only real source of power that we as judges can tap is the respect of the people."

Thurgood Marshall (1908–1993), Supreme Court justice, Chicago Tribune, *August 15, 1981*

"Never expect justice in the world. That is not part of God's plan. Everybody thinks that if they don't get it, they're some kind of odd man out. And it's not true. Nobody gets justice—people get good luck or bad luck."

Orson Welles (1915–1985)

KNOWLEDGE

"Never be afraid of the deafeningly obvious.
It is always news to somebody."

P. J. Kavanagh, A Song and Dance

LAWYERS

"Never look too deep into the mind of a
lawyer."

*Bruce Campbell, as Brisco, "The
Adventures of Brisco County, Jr."*

"Never ask a lawyer or accountant for
business advice. They are trained to find
problems, not solutions."

H. Jackson Brown, Jr.

"Never, ever point your finger at someone."

Attorney Karl Fleming on how to project a good image in the courtroom

LEADERSHIP

"Never tell people *how* to do things. Tell them *what* to do and they will surprise you with their ingenuity."

George S. Patton (1885–1945), U.S. general during World War II, War as I Knew It, *1947*

LEARNING

"Never stop learning."

Motto of the Greater Kansas City YMCA

LENDING

"Never lend any money to anybody unless
they don't need it."

> Ogden Nash (1902–1971)

"Never loan a possession unless you
borrow an item of equal importance at the
same time."

> Steven Kropper, as quoted by Tom
> Parker in Rules of Thumb 2, 1987

LETTERS

"Never write a letter while you are angry."

> Chinese adage

"Never write a letter if you can help it, and never destroy one."

John A. Macdonald

LIFE

"Never take yourself too seriously. Get out that great road map of life and remember: No one, even the most brilliant among you here tonight, will be able to fold it up again."

Kermit the Frog (1958?–), in an address to the Oxford [University] Union Society in England, 1994

"Never yawn or say a commonplace thing,
but burn, burn, burn like fabulous yellow
roman candles exploding like spiders
across the stars and in the middle you see
the blue centerlight pop and everybody
goes 'Awww!'"

   Jack Kerouac (1922–1969)

"Never assume. You never know. You can
never count on life. You can't count on
success. There's just no guarantee. Take it
day to day and enjoy it and be as nice as
you can."

   Sam Kinison (1954–1992)

"Never, for whatever reason, turn your
back on life."

   *Eleanor Roosevelt (1884–1962),
   attributed*

LITERATURE

"Never pursue literature as a trade."

Samuel Taylor Coleridge (1772–1834),
Biographia Literaria, *1817*

"Never write on a subject without having
first read yourself full on it; and never
read on a subject 'till you have thought
yourself hungry on it."

*Jean Paul Friedrich Richter
(1763–1825),* Hesperus, *1795*

LOVE

"Never let a fool kiss you or a kiss fool
you."

Joey Adams (1911–   ), comic

"Never change when love has found its home."

> *Sextus Propertius (54 B.C.–A.D. 2)*

"Never love a stranger."

> *Stella Benson (1892–1933), also the title of a best-selling 1948 Harold Robbins novel*

"Never love unless you can
Bear with all the faults of man."

> *Thomas Campion (1567–1620)*

"Never despise what it says in the women's magazines: it may not be subtle but neither are men."

> *Zsa Zsa Gabor (1917?–   )*

"Never forget that the most powerful force on earth is love."

Nelson Rockefeller (1908–1979), to presidential adviser Henry Kissinger

Lying

"Never tell a lie unless it is absolutely convenient."

Anonymous liar

"Never tell a lie till the truth doesn't fit."

American adage

"Never believe another liar even when you know he's telling the truth."

Laurence J. Peters (1919–1990), Peter's Quotations, 1977

"Never tell a lie to your master or mistress, unless you have some hopes that they cannot find it out."

Jonathan Swift (1667–1745), satiric author and cleric, Directions to Servants

Manners

"Never . . . be half-rude."

Norman Douglas (1868–1952)

"Never drink from your finger bowl—it contains only water."

Addison Mizner (1872–1933), architect, as quoted by Evan Esar in The Dictionary of Humorous Quotations, *1949*

"Never crumble or destroy
Food that others might enjoy. . . ."

> *From "The Little Gentleman," an old*
> *American rhyme, in William J.*
> *Bennett's* The Book of Virtues, *1993*

"Never speak loudly unless the house is
on fire."

> *H. W. Thompson, as quoted by Frank*
> *Pepper in* The Wit and Wisdom of
> the 20th Century, *1987*

"Never be rude to anyone unless you
mean it."

> *Archie Goodwin, assistant to detective*
> *Nero Wolfe, in* Counterfeit for Murder
> *by Rex Stout (1886–1975)*

"Never speak of rope in the house of a man
who has been hanged."

> *Franklin D. Roosevelt (1882–1945)*

"Never try on another man's cowboy hat."

Kristin McMurran, reviewing Way Out West *by Jane and Michael Stern*

MARRIAGE

"Never say that marriage has more of joy
than pain."

> *Euripides (c. 485–406 B.C.)*

"Never marry a widow unless her first
husband was hanged."

> *Scots adage*

"Never advise anyone to go to war or to
marry."

> *Old Spanish adage*

"Never marry a man who hates his mother
because he'll end up hating you."

> *Jill Bennett, attributed, as quoted by
> Abby Adams in* An Uncommon Scold,
> *1989*

"Never get married while you're going to college; it's hard enough to get a start if a prospective employer finds you've already made one mistake."

Frank McKinney "Kin" Hubbard (1868–1930)

"Never confuse 'I love you' with 'I want to marry you.'"

Le Roy King

"Never marry for money. You can borrow it a lot cheaper."

Ann Landers (1918–   )

"Never speak slightingly or bitterly of or to your husband, especially in the presence of other people."

The Old Farmer's Almanac, *1877*

"Never marry but for love; but see that thou lovest what is lovely."

> *William Penn (1644–1718), Some Fruits of Solitude, 1693*

"Never, ever, go to bed angry."

> *Dr. Ruth Westheimer (1928–   )*

"Never go to bed mad. Stay up and fight."

> *Phyllis Diller (1917–   ), Phyllis Diller's Housekeeping Hints*

MEDIA, THE

"Never pick a fight with anyone who buys ink by the barrel."

> *American adage, quoted by Jim Brady (1940–   ), warning politicians against antagonizing newspapers*

"Never question yourself out of a great story."

> *Eddie Clontz, editor of the supermarket tabloid newspaper* Weekly World News, *which covers such stories as Elvis sightings, U.S. senators who are really space aliens, and werewolves in suburbia*

"Never confuse networking with affection. . . . a friendship between reporter and source lasts only until it is profitable for one to betray the other. When the first glimmer hits the horizon that your number is up, your old pals in the press will turn on you and run like the curs they are."

> *Maureen Dowd, journalist*

"Never trust a reporter who has a nice smile."

> *William Rauch (1950–   ), New York City press secretary,* New York Times, *January 18, 1984*

"Never say anything is 'off the record' when speaking to a reporter. . . . There's no such thing. If you don't want what you say to appear on tomorrow's front page, keep your mouth shut."

> *Jeff Slutsky*

"Never lose your temper with the press or the public is a major rule of political life."

> *Christabel Pankhurst (1880–1958), English suffragist,* Unshackled Woman, *1959*

MEN

"Never ask for directions."

From a T-shirt, cited as "The First Rule of Manhood"

"How to Keep Your Man
1. Never put makeup on at the table.
2. Never ask a man where he has been.
3. Never keep him waiting.
4. Never baby him when he is disconsolate.
5. Never fail to baby him when he is sick or has a hangover.
6. Never let him see you when you are not at your best.
7. Never talk about your other dates or boyfriends of the past."

Mae West (1892–1980), who never married successfully

MILITARY, THE

"Never expect a soldier to think."

George Bernard Shaw (1856–1950),
The Devil's Disciple, *1901*

MIMES

"Never get a mime talking. He won't stop."

Marcel Marceau (1923–   ), mime,
U.S. News & World Report,
February 23, 1987

MISFORTUNE

"Never a bad day that hath a good night."

*Anonymous pessimist, seventeenth
century*

"Never find your delight in another's misfortune."

Publilius Syrus (first century B.C.)

MISTAKES

"Never do anything, and you'll never make any mistakes."

Anonymous

"Never say 'oops' in the operating room."

Dr. Leo Troy

MONEY

"Never ask of money spent
Where the spender thinks it went."

> *Robert Frost (1874–1963),* The
> Hardship of Accounting

"Never burn a penny candle looking for a
half-penny."

> *Irish adage*

"Never spend your money before you
have it."

> *Thomas Jefferson (1743–1826),* A
> Decalogue of canons for observation
> in practical life, *in a letter to Thomas
> Jefferson Smith, February 21, 1825
> (Jefferson had severe money troubles.)*

"Never risk more than you can afford to lose."

> *Stockbrokers' adage*

"Never economize on luxuries."

> *Angela Thirkell (1890–1961)*

MOTHERS

"Never compare rotten days with the mother of a toddler."

> *Jerry Scott and Rick Kirkman, Darryl in their comic strip "Baby Blues," July 10, 1994*

"Never introduce a girl named Bubbles to your mother."

> *Burt Reynolds (1936–   )*

"Never tell her about your sex life—or lack of it. It's ugly to see pity in a daughter's eyes."

Joan Rivers (1937–   )

"Never talk about having a fight with your mate. Your mother will automatically hate that person forever."

Melissa Rivers (1969–   )

MOTHERS-IN-LAW

"Never rely on the glory of the morning nor the smiles of your mother-in-law."

Japanese adage

MUSIC

"Never compose anything unless the not composing of it becomes a positive nuisance to you."

Gustav Holst (1874–1934), composer

"Never use a score when conducting. . . . Does a lion tamer enter a cage with a book on how to tame a lion?"

Dimitri Mitropoulos (1896–1960), quoted by Nat Shapiro in Encyclopedia of Quotations About Music

NAÏVETÉ

"Never be naive, no matter how naive you are."

Russell Baker (1925–   ), Bottom Line, September 15, 1993

NATURE

"Never does nature say one thing and wisdom another."

Juvenal (c. 40–125 A.D.), Satires

NEIGHBORS

"Never keep up with the Joneses. Drag them down to your level. It's cheaper."

Quentin Crisp (1910–), British actor and autobiographer

NIGHT

"Never greet a stranger in the night, for he may be a demon."

Talmud

No

"Never say no from pride or yes from weakness."

American adage

"Never take no for an answer from someone who hasn't the authority to say yes."

Anonymous

Opportunity

"Never refuse a good offer."

Anonymous opportunist, seventeenth century

Others

"Never idealize others. They will never live up to your expectations."

Leo Buscaglia (1924–   )

Parties

"Never ask what you did; it's better not to know."

Peter O'Toole (1932–   ), notorious for his wild partying, as quoted by his drinking buddy Michael Caine (1933–   ) in What's It All About?, *1992*

PAST, THE

"Never look for birds of this year in the
nests of the last."

> *Miguel de Cervantes (1547–1616),*
> Don Quixote de la Mancha

"Never look back; look forward. You've got
to have something to live for, otherwise
you cease to live. And who wants to live
when you have nothing to live for?"

> *Richard Nixon (1913–1994), on his*
> *eightieth birthday*

PERFECTIONISM

"Never get a reputation for a small perfection, if you are trying for fame in a loftier area. The world can only judge by generals, and it sees that those who pay considerable attention to the minutiae, seldom have their minds occupied with great things."

Edward Bulwer-Lytton (1803–1873)

"Never expect to see perfect work from imperfect man."

Alexander Hamilton (1757–1804), The Federalist, edited by Benjamin F. Wright, 1961

PERSISTENCE

"Never say die."

> *An adage used by Charles Dickens*
> *(1812–1870) in his* Pickwick Papers,
> *1836–1837*

"Never give in, never give in, never, never,
never, never—in nothing, great or small,
large or petty—never give in except to
convictions of honor and good sense."

> *Winston Churchill (1874–1965), an*
> *address at Harrow School October 29,*
> *1941*

"Never give in, never, never, never give in."

> *H. Ross Perot (1930–   ), para-*
> *phrasing Winston Churchill shortly*
> *before temporarily bowing out of the*
> *1992 presidential race*

PLANNING

"Never plan the future by the past."

Edmund Burke (1729–1797), letter to a member of the National Assembly, 1721

POKER

"Never chase a hand. Fold a seven card stud hand if you don't start with at least a pair, three cards of the same suit or the middle three cards of a straight. Fold a draw poker hand if you don't have a pair of jacks or better."

Steve Fox, executive director, National Poker Association

POLITICS

"Never hold discussions with the monkey
when the organ grinder is in the room."

Winston Churchill (1874–1965),
attributed

"Never vote for the best candidate; vote for
the one who will do the least harm."

Frank Dane

"Never judge a country by its politics. After
all, we English are quite honest by nature,
aren't we?"

Alfred Hitchcock (1899–1980), The
Lady Vanishes, *1938*

"Never be afraid to stand with the minority when the minority is right, for the minority which is right will one day be the majority."

> *William Jennings Bryan (1860–1925),*
> *"Cast Your Vote"*

"Never believe anything until it's been officially denied."

> *Antony Jay (1930–) and Jonathan*
> *Lynn (1943–), Yes, Prime*
> *Minister, volume 1*

"Never take notice of anonymous letters, unless you get a few thousand on the same subject."

> *Robert Gordon Menzies (1895–1978),*
> *Australian prime minister (1939–1941,*
> *1949–1966), as quoted by Jonathon*
> *Green in* The Book of Political
> Quotes, *1982*

"Never play cards with any man named Doc."

Nelson Algren (1909–1981),
Newsweek, July 2, 1956

"Never underestimate the ability of the Democrats to wet their finger and hold it to the wind."

Ronald Reagan (1911–   ),
Newsweek, July 10, 1978

"Never forget that government is *ourselves* and not an alien power over us. The ultimate rulers of our democracy are not a president and senators and congressmen and government officials but the voters of this country."

Franklin D. Roosevelt (1882–1945)

"Never doubt that a small group of committed citizens can change the world. Indeed, it is the only thing that ever has."

Margaret Mead (1901–1978)

"Never blame a legislative body for not doing something. When they do nothing, they don't hurt anybody. When they do something is when they become dangerous."

Will Rogers (1879–1935), as quoted by Richard Ketchum in Will Rogers: His Life and Times, *1973*

"Never underestimate the ability of a politician to (a) say something and tell you not very much, (b) do it with style, and (c) touch all the bases."

Robert H. Williams, journalist, Washington Post

PRIDE

"Never be haughty to the humble; never be
humble to the haughty."

> *Jefferson Davis (1808–1889), who
> fought a war to preserve slavery*

"Never be too proud to turn back."

> *American adage*

PRINCIPLES

"Never stand so high upon a principle that
you cannot lower it to suit the
circumstances."

> *Winston Churchill (1874–1965)*

PROBLEMS

"Never does the course of true anything
run smooth."

Samuel Butler, attributed

"Never let life's hardships disturb you. After
all, no one can avoid problems, not even
saints or sages."

Nichiren Daishonin (1222–1282),
The Major Writings of Nichiren
Daishonin: Happiness in this World

"Never deal with the flyweights of the
world. They take far too much pleasure in
thwarting you at every turn."

*Sue Grafton (1940–   ), mystery
writer, "H" is for Homicide, 1990*

PROCRASTINATION

"Never put off till tomorrow that which you can do today."

An old proverb dating to the fourteenth century, popularized by Benjamin Franklin (1706–1790)

"Never put off till tomorrow what you can do today. You might like it, and then you can do it again tomorrow."

Anonymous

"Never put off till tomorrow what you can get someone else to do today."

Anonymous

"Never do today what you can do tomorrow. Something may occur to make you regret your premature action."

> *Aaron Burr (1757–1836), also attributed to many others*

"Never put off until tomorrow what you can manage to wriggle out of today."

> *Doug Larson*

"Never put off until tomorrow what you can do the day after tomorrow."

> *Mark Twain (Samuel Clemens) (1835–1910)*

"Never put off until tomorrow what can be avoided altogether."

> *Ann Landers (1918–   ), 1994*

"Never delay kissing a pretty girl or opening a bottle of whiskey."

Ernest Hemingway (1899–1961), as quoted by Carlos Baker, Ernest Hemingway: A Life Story, *1968*

PROMISES

"Never make a promise which you do not fulfill."

Winston Churchill (1874–1965)

"Never promise more than you can perform."

Publilius Syrus (first century B.C.)

PROPHECY

"Never prophesy—onless ye know."

> *James Russell Lowell (1819–1891)*

"Never prophesy, for if you prophesy
wrong, nobody will forget it, and if you
prophesy right, nobody will remember it."

> *Josh Billings (Henry Wheeler Shaw)
> (1818–1885), humorist*

PUBLIC RELATIONS

"Never characterize the importance of a
statement in advance."

> *Charles G. Ross (1885–1950), press
> secretary to Harry Truman*

PUNCTUALITY

"Never arrive on time; this stamps you as a beginner."

Harry Chapman

QUESTIONS

"Never answer a question, other than an offer of marriage, by saying Yes or No."

Susan Chitty, The Intelligent Woman's Guide to Good Taste, *1958*

"Never be afraid of asking a dumb question. It beats making a dumb mistake."

Anonymous

"Never, never, never, on cross-examination ask a witness a question you don't already know the answer to, was a tenet I absorbed with my babyfood. Do it, and you'll often get an answer you don't want, an answer that might wreck your case."

Atticus Finch, in To Kill a Mockingbird, 1960, *by Harper Lee (1926–   )*

"Never answer a question until it is asked."

Lawyer's adage

REAL ESTATE

"Never build after you are five and forty; have five years' income in hand before you lay a brick; and always calculate the expense at double the estimate."

Henry Kett

REASON

"Never get angry, never make a threat.
Reason with people."

Marlon Brando, as Don Corleone in
The Godfather, *1972*

"Never try to reason the prejudice out of a
man. It was not reasoned into him, and
cannot be reasoned out."

Sydney Smith (1771–1845)

"Never use . . . reason against truth."

*Elie Wiesel (1928–   ), quoting from
a Hasidic prayer*

REGRET

"Never . . . regret and never look back. Regret is an appalling waste of energy; you can't build on it; it's good only for wallowing in."

Katherine Mansfield (1888–1923), New Zealand–born English author, Bliss, *1923*

"Never look back. We all live in suspense, from day to day, from hour to hour; in other words, we are the hero of our own story."

Mary McCarthy (1912–1989)

REPAIRS

"Never sew a new patch on an old garment."

American adage

RESTAURANTS

"Never order chicken-fried steak in a place that doesn't have a jukebox."

H. Jackson Brown, Jr.

"Never eat in a restaurant where there's a photo of the chef with Sammy Davis, Jr."

Alf, on "Alf"

"Never eat at any place called 'Mom's.'"

Nelson Algren (1909–1981), quoting advice given to him by a convict, Newsweek, *July 2, 1956*

"Never eat in a restaurant that's over a hundred feet off the ground and won't stand still."

> *Calvin Trillin (1935–   ), food critic,* Interview, December 29, 1979

"Never eat Chinese food in Oklahoma."

> *Bryan Miller, "Never Eat at Mom's,"* New York Times, July 16, 1983

"Never eat in an empty restaurant. Everybody who's not there must know something."

> *Jim Quinn,* But Never Eat Out on a Saturday Night

"Never piss off the person who is handling what you are putting in your mouth."

> *A waiter at L.A.'s posh eatery Spago, attributed*

ROMANCE

"Never flirt with a woman whose husband carries a gun."

> *George Wyner, as assistant district attorney Irwin Berstein in "Hill Street Blues"*

"Never let your beloved get accustomed to your absence."

> *Lucas Cleeve, attributed*

"Never trust a husband too far nor a bachelor too near."

> *Helen Rowland (1876–1950), journalist*

RURAL AREAS

"Never drive through a small southern town at 100 mph with the local sheriff's drunken 16-year-old daughter on your lap naked."

Anonymous member of a chain gang

SAFETY

"Never cry wolf when not in danger."

Anonymous

"Never take medicines in the dark."

Linda F. Golodner, president, National Consumers League, 1994

"Never use while sleeping."

*Hair dryer instruction accompanying
Conair hair dryers, 1993*

"Never rock or tilt. Vending machine will
not dispense free product."

*Safety instruction placed on soda
machines after dozens of people were
killed by soda machines that fell over
and crushed them after being rocked or
tilted*

SALESMANSHIP

"Never offer your hen for sale on a rainy
day."

*Spanish adage, meaning that a good
appearance helps sell a product—a wet
hen looks small and miserable*

"Never say no when a client asks for something—even if it is the moon. You can always try, and anyhow there is plenty of time afterward to explain that it was not possible."

> *Caesar Ritz, Swiss founder of the Ritz Hotel empire, who began his career as a cowherd*

"Never simply say, 'Sorry, we don't have what you are looking for.' Always say, 'Too bad, I just sold one the other day.'"

> *Robert Skole*

SCANDAL

"Never get caught in bed with a live man or a dead woman."

> *Larry Hagman as J. R. Ewing, Jr., in "Dallas"*

SECRECY

"Never participate in the secrets of those above you; you think you share the fruit, and you share the stones. . . . the confidence of a prince is not a grant, but a tax."

Baltasar Gracián (1601–1658)

"Never trust anyone with a secret, except your mother."

Irene Zahava

Self-Defense

"Never, never adhere to the Christian belief of turning the other cheek. That is for weak people. You cannot allow a direct challenge to go unanswered; an affront demands a reaction—and don't listen to women when they try to dissuade you from fighting. You must defend your honor."

> *Colonel Zboromirski, an ex-officer of the czar's Imperial Guards hired to tutor the young Oleg Cassini, as quoted in Cassini's* In My Own Fashion, *1987*

"Never volunteer."

U.S. Army adage

"Never, *ever* forget that people's selfish interest comes first, and that includes you and me. Doing what we feel we have to do for ourselves—even if inconvenient to others—is how we stay alive and occasionally get something we want. Underneath—possibly *way* underneath baffling behavior—is the likelihood the behavior is answering somebody's (dumb or reasonable) need. *Live* with that."

Helen Gurley Brown (1922–   ),
"Getting It," Cosmopolitan, *July 1994*

"Never fall out with your bread and butter."

English adage

"Never give a sucker an even break, or smarten up a chump."

W. C. Fields (1879–1946), also
attributed to Edward Francis Albee
(1857–1930)

SELF-RELIANCE

"Never trouble another for what you can do for yourself."

> *Thomas Jefferson (1743–1826), A Decalogue of canons for observation in practical life, in a letter to Thomas Jefferson Smith, February 21, 1825*

"Never let anybody walk all over you."

> *Michael Landon (1937–1991), as quoted by Shannen Doherty, People Weekly, November 9, 1992*

"Never grow a wishbone, daughter, where your backbone ought to be."

> *Clementine Paddleford (1900–1967), food editor and columnist*

SELF-RESPECT

"Never esteem anything as of advantage to you that will make you break your word or lose your self-respect."

Marcus Aurelius Antoninus (121–180),
Roman emperor, Meditations

SENTIMENT

"Never let sentiment get into the way of your work."

A Cardassian about to murder a
former friend in "Deep Space Nine"

SEX

Never Make Love in a Suit of Armor

> *Title of a book by Michael Green, 1983*

"Never die for love or anything remotely resembling it."

> *Norman Mailer (1923–   ), stating, in a 1994* Esquire *interview with Madonna, what he thinks is the hidden message in condom usage*

Never Sleep with a Fat Man in July

> *Title of a book by Modine Gunch, 1993*

"Never talk in the bedroom—except on the phone."

> *Marilyn Monroe (1926–1962)*

"Never advertise what you don't have for
sale."

> *Anonymous mother, as quoted by*
> *Michele Slung in* More Momilies, *1986*

SHORTNESS

"Never trust a man with short legs—brains
too near their bottoms."

> *Noel Coward (1899–1973)*

SILENCE

"Never mistake silence for consent."

> *English adage*

"And never, never, no matter what else you do in your whole life, *never* sleep with anyone whose troubles are worse than your own."

Nelson Algren (1909–1981),
Newsweek, *July 2, 1956*

"Never assume that habitual silence means ability in reserve."

> *Geoffrey Madan,* Twelve Reflections, *1934*

SISTERS

"Never praise a sister to a sister, in the hope of your compliments reaching the proper ears."

> *Rudyard Kipling (1865–1936), "False Dawn,"* Plain Tales from the Hills, *1888*

Sleep

"Never waste any time you could spend sleeping."

> *Frank Knight, professor of economics,*
> *University of Chicago, as quoted by*
> *Benjamin J. Stein*

"Never nap after a meal or you'll get fat."

> *Anonymous mother, as quoted by*
> *Michele Slung in* Momilies, *1985*

Soap Operas

"Never tell today what you can put off till tomorrow."

> *Agnes Nixon, prolific soap opera writer*

SPEECH

"Never waste space saying, 'On the one hand.' Just state an opinion in a Godlike voice."

> *Arthur Christiansen (d. 1963), editor of the* London Daily Express, *in the* New York Herald Tribune, *September 28, 1963*

"Never say nothin' without you're compelled tu. . . . then don't say nothin' thet you can be held tu."

> *James Russell Lowell (1819–1891),* The Biglow Papers, *1848*

"Never say anything remarkable. It is sure to be wrong."

> *Mark Rutherford [William Hale White] (1831–1913), British writer,* Last Pages from a Journal, *1915*

"Never say more than is necessary."

Richard Brinsley Sheridan
(1751–1816)

"Never hold any one by the button, or the hand, in order to be heard out; for if people are unwilling to hear you, you had better hold your tongue than them."

Fourth Earl of Chesterfield (Philip Dormer Stanhope) (1694–1773)

"Never try to tell everything you know. It may take too short a time."

Norman Ford (1921–   )

"Never speak of yourself to others; make them talk about themselves instead: therein lies the whole art of pleasing."

Jules de Goncourt (1830–1870)

"Never impose your language on people you wish to reach."

> *Abbie Hoffman (1937–1989),*
> Revolution for the Hell of It, *1968*

SPORTS

"Never agree to play tennis for money against a gray-haired player."

> *Tom Robinson, as quoted by Tom Parker in* Rules of Thumb 2, *1987*

"Never precede any maneuver by a comment more predictive than 'Watch this!' (Keep 'em guessing.)"

> *Dan "The Stork" Roddick, editor of* Frisbee World *and director of the International Frisbee Association*

"Never race a guy named Flash."

Burt Reynolds (1936–)

"Never jog. Love is still a better and more pleasurable sport."

Cary Grant (1904–1986)

STABILITY

"Never swap horses midstream."

American adage

"Never needlesly disturb a thing at rest."

John Randolph (1773–1833), U.S. statesman

"Never confuse stability with stagnation."

Mary Jean Le Tendre (1948–   ),
educator, as quoted in The Last Word
by Carolyn Warner

STATISTICS

"Never try to walk across a river just
because it has an average depth of four
feet."

Milton Friedman (1912–   )

"Never be the man in the chair—be the man behind the man in the chair."

Gangland adage

STRATEGY

"Never hunt rabbit with dead dog."

> *Charlie Chan, the creation of mystery writer Earl Derr Biggers (1884–1933), as quoted in* Quotations from Charlie Chan (1968), *edited by Harvey Chertok and Martha Torge*

"Never chase a man over a cliff."

> *Paul Gross, as Benton Fraiser, RCMP, quoting his father in "Due South"*

"Never send a polliwog to tackle a whale."

> *Abraham Lincoln (1809–1865)*

"Never tell them what you wouldn't do."

> *Adam Clayton Powell, Jr. (1908–1972), U.S. congressman*

"Never murder a man when he's busy committing suicide."

> Woodrow Wilson (1856–1924), *letter to Bernard Baruch, 1916*

"Never from obstinancy take the wrong side because your opponent has anticipated you in taking the right side."

> *Balthasar Gracián (1601–1658)*

"Never tell your resolution beforehand."

> *John Selden,* Table Talk, *c. 1650*

STRENGTH

"Never give up: and never, under any circumstances, no matter what—never face the facts."

> *Ruth Gordon (1896–1985)*

"Never let them see you cry . . . suck it up
and go in there and try to be yourself."

> *Deborah Norville (1958–   ),
> television journalist*

"Never let your head hang down. Never
give up and sit down and grieve. Find
another way. And don't pray when it rains
if you don't pray when the sun shines."

> *Satchel Paige (1906–1982)*

SUCCESS

"Never lose sight of the fact that the most
important yardstick of your success will
be how you treat other people—your
family, friends, and coworkers, and even
strangers you meet along the way."

> *Barbara Bush (1925–   )*

"Never give up. A little money helps, but what really gets it right is to never . . . under any conditions face the facts."

Ruth Gordon (1896–1985)

TELEPHONE

"Never say anything on the phone that you wouldn't want your mother to hear at your trial."

Sydney Biddle Barrows, the "Mayflower madam," as quoted by Marian Christy in " 'Mayflower Madam' Tells All," Boston Globe, September 10, 1986

"Never answer a telephone that rings before breakfast. It is sure to be one of three types of persons: a strange man in Minneapolis who has been up all night and is phoning collect; a salesman who wants to come over and demonstrate a combination Dictaphone and music box that also cleans rugs; or a woman out of one's past."

James Thurber (1894–1961)

TELEVISION

"Never underestimate the poor taste of the public."

Anonymous TV executive

"Never miss a chance to have sex or appear on television."

Gore Vidal (1925–   )

TEMPTATION

"Never stop to argue with temptation."

American adage

"Never resist temptation: prove all things:
hold fast that which is good."

George Bernard Shaw (1856–1950),
Maxims for Revolutionists

TEXAS

"Never ask a man if he's from Texas. If he
is, he'll tell you. If he ain't, no need to
embarrass him."

*Anonymous Texan giving advice to
his son*

THINGS

"Never fight an inanimate object."

P. J. O'Rourke (1947–   )

THOUGHT

"Never be afraid to sit awhile and think."

Lorraine Hansberry (1930–1965),
A Raisin in the Sun, 1959

THREATS

"Never, ever, threaten unless you're going to follow through, because if you don't, the next time you won't be taken seriously."

Roy M. Cohn (1927–1986)

TOBACCO

"Never smoke more than one cigar at a time."

> *Mark Twain (Samuel L. Clemens) (1835–1910)*

"Never slap a man who chews tobacco."

> *Willard Scott (1934–   )*

TRAVEL

"Never take no cutoffs. And hurry along."

> *Virginia Reed, one of the few survivors of the Donner Party of 1847, which had taken a cutoff and hadn't hurried along as fast as they should have and wound up eating each other*

"Never attempt to fire a gun or pistol while on the road; it may frighten the team and the careless handling and cocking of the weapon makes nervous people nervous. Don't discuss politics or religion, nor point out places on the road where horrible murders have been committed, if delicate women are among the passengers."

> "Stagecoach Etiquette," Omaha
> Herald, *as quoted in Marc
> McCutcheon's* The Writer's Guide to
> Everyday Life in the 1800s, *1993*

"Never be flippantly rude to elderly strangers in foreign hotels. They always turn out to be the King of Sweden."

> *Saki (Hector Hugh Munro)
> (1870–1916)*

TRUST

"Never trust the advice of a man in
difficulties."

> *Aesop (fl. c. 550 B.C.)*

"Never trust a hot head or a cold heart."

> *Anonymous*

"Never trust a wolf's tameness, a horse's
health, or an enemy's smile."

> *Darby Hinton as Israel Boone in
> "Daniel Boone"*

"Never trust anyone who can't sing
harmony."

> *George Burns (1896–   ), The Third
> Time Around, 1980*

"Never trust a man with a small cock."

Jean Cocteau (1891–1963)

"Never trust a man who speaks well of everybody."

– *John Churton Collins (1848–1908)*

"Never trust a man with a tattoo on his face."

Johnny Hart (1931–   ), in his comic strip "B.C."

"Never Trust the Man who hath reason to suspect that you know he hath injured you."

Henry Fielding (1707–1754)

"Never trust a man unless you've got his pecker in your pocket."

Lyndon Baines Johnson (1908–1973), attributed

"Never trust a man whose eyes are too close to his nose."

Lyndon Baines Johnson (1908–1973)

"Never trust a man who combs his hair straight from his left armpit."

Alice Roosevelt Longworth (1884–1980), describing Douglas MacArthur, Michael Teague, Mrs. L: Conversations with Alice Roosevelt Longworth, *1981*

"Never trust a man with a small black mustache."

P. G. Wodehouse (1881–1975)

TRUTH

"Never wear your best trousers when you go out to fight for freedom and truth."

> *Henrik Ibsen (1828–1906),* An Enemy of the People

"Never accept any statement or even fact as being the absolute truth. . . . No statement should be believed merely because it has been made by an authority."

> *Hans Reichenbach (1891–1953)*

"Never tell the truth to people who are not worthy of it."

> *Mark Twain (Samuel Clemens) (1835–1910)*

VACATIONS

"Never take vacations
To visit relations."

Gerald Barzan

VICE

"Never practice two vices at once."

Tallulah Bankhead (1902–1968),
Tallulah

"Never trust a man who has not a single
redeeming vice."

Winston Churchill (1874–1965)

"Never support two weaknesses at the same time. It's your combination sinners—your lecherous liars and your miserly drunkards—who dishonor the vices and bring them into disrepute."

> *Thornton Wilder (1897–1975),*
> The Matchmaker, *1955*

VOTING

"Never vote *for* anyone . . . vote against."

> *W. C. Fields (1879–1946)*

WAR

"Never, never, never believe any war will be smooth and easy, or that anyone who embarks on the strange voyage can measure the tides and hurricanes he will encounter. The statesman who yields to the war fever must realize that once the signal is given, he is no longer the master of policy."

Winston Churchill (1874–1965)

WEAKNESS

"Never show your wounded finger, for everything will knock up against it."

Baltasar Gracián (1601–1658)

WEATHER

"Never use the plumbing during a
thunderstorm."

*Anonymous mother, as quoted by
Michele Slung in* Momilies, *1985*

WHIMS

"Never lose sight of the fact that all human
felicity lies in man's imagination, and that
he cannot think to attain it unless he
heeds all his caprices. The most fortunate
of persons is he who has the most means
to satisfy his vagaries."

*Marquise de Sade (1740–1814), French
author, Saint-Fond, in* L'Histoire de
Juliette, ou les Prospérités du Vice,
1797

WINE

"Never buy a case until you've tried at least one bottle."

Frank J. Prial

WIVES

"Ne'er take a wife till thou hast a house to put her in."

Benjamin Franklin (1706–1790),
Poor Richard's Almanac, 1733

"Never feel remorse for what you have thought about your wife; she has thought much worse things about you."

Jean Rostand (1894–1977),
Le Mariage, 1927

"Never judge a man by the opinion his wife
has of him."

> *Bob Edwards (d. 1922), Canadian
> journalist*

WOMEN

"Never . . . comment on a woman's rear
end. Never use the words large or size
with rear end. Never. Avoid the area
altogether. Trust me."

> *Tim Allen (1953–   )*

"Never praise a woman for having
masculine qualities."

> *English adage*

"Never tell a woman she doesn't look good in some article of clothing she has just purchased."

Lewis Grizzard (1946–1994)

"Never try to impress a woman, because if you do she'll expect you to keep up to the standard for the rest of your life."

W. C. Fields (1879–1946)

"Never trust a lady who mentions her virtue."

French adage

"Never judge a woman by the company she is compelled to entertain."

Bob Edwards (d. 1922), Canadian journalist

"Never trust a woman, even if she has borne you seven children."

Japanese adage

"Never try to outsmart a woman, unless you are another woman."

William Lyon Phelps (1865–1943)

"Never give a woman anything she can't wear in the evening."

> *Oscar Wilde (1854–1900)*

"Never have yourself tattooed with any woman's name, not even her initials."

> *P. G. Wodehouse (1881–1975)*

WORK

"Never work before breakfast; if you have to work before breakfast, get your breakfast first."

> *Josh Billings (Henry Wheeler Shaw) (1818–1885)*

"Never take a job where the boss calls you 'Babe.'"

> *Brett Butler (1958–   ), as Grace Kelly in "Grace Under Fire"*

Never Read a Newspaper at Your Desk

> *Title of a book on business behavior by Richard Stiegele, 1994*

"Never stop, except occasionally to put a fork in your mouth."

> *John Walcott,* Times, *April 30, 1985*

"Never keep your hands in your pockets."

> *Michael Korda (1933–   )*

"Never do a job where you can be replaced by a machine."

> *Maurice Joseph Micklewhite, a porter at London's Billingsgate fish market, as quoted by his son Michael Caine (1933–   ), in* What's It All About?, *1992*

"Never start a project until you've picked out someone to blame."

Johnny Hart and Brent Parker, in their comic strip "The Wizard of Id"

"Never take a job where winter winds can blow up your pants."

> *Geraldo Rivera (1943–   ), explaining why he hated a boyhood job delivering newspapers on Long Island in his book* Exposing Myself, 1992

"Never buy anything with a handle on it. It means work."

> *H. Allen Smith (1907–1976)*

"Never allow your sense of self to become associated with your sense of job. If your job vanishes, your self doesn't."

> *Gordon Van Sauter,* Working Woman, *February 1988*

WRITING AND WRITERS

"Never use a long word where a short one would answer the purpose. I know there are professors in this country who 'ligate' arteries. Other surgeons only tie them, and it stops the bleeding just as well."

Oliver Wendell Holmes (1809–1894), in a lecture at Harvard University, November 6, 1867

"Never write anything down, and never throw away anything that other people have written down."

Maureen Dowd, journalist

"Never let a domestic quarrel ruin a day's writing. If you can't start the next day fresh, get rid of your wife."

Mario Puzo (1920–   ), on one of his rules for writing a bestseller

Never Put It in Writing

>*Title of a 1964 movie*

"Never trust a man who has only one way to spell a word."

>*Dan Quayle (1947–   ), quoting Mark Twain*

YOUTH

"Never trust the advice of anyone who gets his information from comic books."

>*Anonymous*

"Never speak of any time of youth as being unhappy. Stupid perhaps, but not unhappy."

>*Adam Wheeler*

"Never try to joke with young people
because it'll just confirm their suspicion
that old people are crazy."

Russell Baker (1925–   )

Ze End

"Never say never."

Anonymous

End Note

I hope you have enjoyed this collection of quotations. If your favorite "Never . . ." quotation was omitted, please send it (along with the name of its author and where you found the quote) to be included in a sequel to this book. The first person to submit a quote will be acknowledged if the quote is used.

Send your quote to:

Ed Morrow
c/o Contemporary Books, Inc.
Two Prudential Plaza, Suite 1200
Chicago, Illinois 60601-6790